11+
Verbal Activity

Technique for CEM Style Questions

WORKBOOK 3

Dr Stephen C Curran
with Katrina MacKay & Autumn McMahon
Edited by Andrea Richardson

This book belongs to

Accelerated Education Publications Ltd

Contents

8. Classification   **Pages**

1. Odd One Out   3-7
2. Synonyms   8-11
3. Antonyms   12-16
4. Homonyms   16-19

9. Cloze

1. Multiple-choice   20-28
2. Word Bank   28-33
3. Missing Letters   34-39

10. Syntax

1. Words Changing Places   40-42
2. Basic Ordering   42-44
3. Selecting a Specific Word   44-45
4. Selecting the Extra Word   45-47

11. Comprehension

1. Fiction & Non-fiction   48-50
2. Forms of Prose   51-55
3. Comprehension Skills   56
4. The Five W's   56-61
5. The Three Question Types   62-67

© 2017 Stephen Curran

Chapter Eight
CLASSIFICATION

Classification involves working out the meanings of words. Once the meanings of the words have been understood, they can be separated into their correct groupings. This applies to any form of grouping, including objects, meanings of words, ideas and subject areas.

An example of a simple classification (grouping) of animals:
- mammals have hair or fur (e.g. cat, horse)
- reptiles have scales (e.g. alligator, snake)
- birds have feathers and wings (e.g. eagle, sparrow)
- amphibians live on land and in water (e.g. frog, toad)
- fish breathe underwater using gills (e.g. shark, salmon)

Work connected with classification requires excellent spelling and vocabulary skills. Working through the Spelling & Vocabulary workbooks will develop these skills.

The following question types involve classification:

Odd One Out • Synonyms • Antonyms • Homonyms

1. Odd One Out

Odd One Out involves finding the word that does not belong to the group. This is done by deciding what the particular grouping is and which word does not fit into this grouping. There are a number of different types of odd one out question:

Noun Grouping • Word Play • Word Meanings

Example: Identify the word that does not fit into the group.
playmate   rival   friend   ally   classmate

1. Try and decide what the grouping is. This may be hard as the meanings of all the words may not be known. This grouping seems to be about friendship.
Playmate, **friend**, **ally** and **classmate** all mean to be friends with another person.

2. Look for the word that does not fit into this particular classification. **Rival** means a person or thing that competes with another for the same outcome. This must be the odd one out as it is harder to be friends with someone if you are competing over something.

The odd one out is: rival

a. Noun Grouping

This type of Odd One Out question is about deciding on the group a noun might belong to. A noun is a name for a person, place or thing, e.g. oboe, flute, piccolo, clarinet and bassoon are all names of wind instruments.

Exercise 8: 1   Underline the odd one out:

1) second   minute   hour   day   metre

2) goat   lion   sheep   horse   cow

3) ferry   submarine   canoe   plane   kayak

4) car   farm   zoo   funfair   circus

5)   arithmetic   school   English   chemistry   art

6)   French   Irish   English   Germany   Indian

7)   December   October   Tuesday   April   November

8)   flamingo   owl   swan   wren   butterfly

9)   banana   cauliflower   potato   cabbage   pea

10) palace   cottage   shop   flat   castle

Score

b. Word Play

This type of Odd One Out question is about how words are put together, not what the words mean. It includes the following types:

- Matching Letters – a group of words that contain the same letters or combinations of letters, e.g. flee<u>ing</u> and buy<u>ing</u>.

- Palindromes – words that read the same forwards and backwards, e.g. madam

- Rhyming Words – words that have the same sound or end with the same sound, e.g. note and boat.

- Silent Letters – words that contain letters that are not sounded when they are spoken, e.g. dum<u>b</u> and <u>g</u>naw.

- Semordnilaps – words that will spell another word backwards, e.g. tip spells pit backwards.

Exercise 8: 2 Underline the odd one out:

1) live   close   bow   tear   twist

2) saw   wage   loot   tide   won

3) wharf   whisper   wheelchair   window   wheat

4) aim   train   game   fame   claim

5) madam   racecar   read   toot   minim

6) buy   try   cry   fly   joy

7) gnaw   arrow   meadow   rainbow   yellow

8) permit   eagle   rear   label   thought

9) climb   rhythm   thumb   match   womb

10) butterfly   sky   many   pigsty   buy

c. Word Meanings

In this type of Odd One Out question all but one of the words have similar meanings (synonyms).

For example, funny, humorous, comical, hilarious and hysterical all have similar meanings.

Exercise 8: 3 Underline the odd one out:

1) turn   spin   twirl   whirl   straight

2) brilliant   fantastic   great   big   terrific

3) spoil   dirty   earth   soil   ruin

4) funny <u>usual</u> strange weird odd

5) sad merry jolly happy glad

6) rug curtain carpet mat flooring

7) rubbish trash good junk waste

8) present gift reward past award

9) irritated mad angry furious happy

10) sack plastic bag backpack rucksack

d. Mixed Examples

Exercise 8: 4   Underline the odd one out:

1) ran caught said talking saw

2) he she we they person

3) quick fast slow rapid swift

4) may part pit fits swap

5) kind type gentle caring thoughtful

6) anger love smile grief fear

7) unused new fresh aged pristine

8) chaffinch flipper mallet survivor yellow

9) Autumn Monday Thursday Sunday Saturday

10) widow demand health mirror toast

© 2017 Stephen Curran

2. Synonyms

A **Synonym** is a word that has a similar meaning to another word. There are two types of synonym question:

Select the Synonym • **Spell the Synonym**

a. Select the Synonym

Example: Which one of the following words is a synonym of the word **murmur**?

shout   scream   utter   shriek

1. Try to decide the meaning of the key word **murmur**. **Murmur** means to say something that is not easily heard.
2. Compare the meanings of each word with the word **murmur**.
   - **shout** means to say something loudly. This word does mean to say something but it is not quiet.
   - **scream** means to give a long, loud cry, but no words are spoken.
   - **shriek** means to scream. This is a high pitched noise without speech.
3. Only **utter** remains. **Utter** means to say something quietly. This word compares well with the meaning of **murmur**, which also means to speak quietly.
4. Check if both words fit into the same sentence.
   'I heard a voice murmur something in my ear.'
   'I heard a voice utter something in my ear.'
   Both of these words work in this sentence.

The correct synonym is: utter

Exercise 8: 5

Underline the word which is a synonym of the word in bold:

Score

1) **hyphen** rush   dash   hurry   stop

2) **ghost**   phantom   person   air   grey

3) **meadow** stream   field   green   grass

4) **drain**   hole   water   gutter   rain

5) **shoreline**   sand   coast   rocks   cliff

6) **grave**   silly   fun   main   serious

7) **pair**   pear   match   both   too

8) **rage**   annoy   fury   angry   irate

9) **slave**   servant   worker   person   employee

10) **answer**   question   speech   reply   talk

b. Spell the Synonym

Example: Complete the word on the right by filling in the missing letters. It is a synonym of the word on the left.

beak   b ☐ ☐ 1

1. Think about the word on the left and its meaning. A **beak** is part of a bird's jaw. This will give a clue to the word on the right.

© 2017 Stephen Curran

9

2. There is likely to be a vowel after the first letter and there are only five of these – **a**, **e**, **i**, **o** and **u**. These letters could be tried out.

b	a		l
b	e		l
b	i		l
b	o		l
b	u		l

3. Try out letters from the alphabet in the remaining space. The letter **l** can only follow certain letters in a word. Two likely possibilities are **ll** and **wl**. These letters could be tried out to make words.

b	a	l	l		b	i	l	l		b	a	w	l
b	e	l	l		b	u	l	l		b	o	w	l

4. Look for the word that means the same as **beak**. The word **bill** means a bird's **beak**.

The correct synonym is: bill

Exercise 8: 6 Complete the word on the right by filling in the missing letters. It is a synonym of the word on the left:

1) **well-known** | f | a | m | | | s |

2) **baby** | | n | f | | n | t |

3) **look** | g | | | n | c | e |

4) **comb** | b | | u | s | |

5) **soldiers** | t | r | | | p | s |

6) **laugh**	g	g		l	e
7) **wait**	p	a		s	
8) **port**	h	a		b		r
9) **shock**	s		a		e
10) **stove**	c			k	e	

Score

c. Mixed Examples

Exercise 8: 7 Complete or underline the word on the right that is a synonym of the word on the left:

1) **spoil**   improve ruin increase decrease

2) **tutor**   assistant helper teacher worker

3) **circular**   round globe ball sphere

4) **buccaneer**   ship cargo maid pirate

5) **cured**   ill worse better healed

6) **begin** | s | | a | | t |

7) **rip** | t | | r |

8) **fool** | c | l | | | n |

9) **strange** | w | | r | d |

10) **wonderful** | t | e | | r | | f | | c |

Score

© 2017 Stephen Curran

3. Antonyms

An **Antonym** is a word that is opposite in meaning to another word. There are two types of antonym question:

Select the Antonym • **Spell the Antonym**

a. Select the Antonym

Example: Which one of the following words is an antonym of the word **stop**?

> still   continue   carry   end

1. Try to decide the meaning of the key word **stop**. To **stop** means something has come to a finish.

2. Compare the meanings of each word with **stop**.

   - **still** describes something that does not move.
   - **carry** means to move something from one place to another. This has nothing to do with stopping.
   - **end** means to finish. This is a synonym of **stop**.

3. Only **continue** remains. To **continue** means to carry on. This is the opposite of stopping and looks like the correct answer.

4. Check if both words fit into the same sentence.
   'Would you like to stop?'
   'Would you like to continue?'
   Both of these words work in this sentence.

The correct antonym is: continue

Exercise 8: 8

Underline the word which is an antonym of the word in bold:

Score

1) **leap**   crouch   jump   spring   move

2) **above**   over   high   below   up

3) **release**   free   capture   rent   lease

4) **cool**   warm   chilly   cold   calm

5) **deny**   lie   admit   disagree   object

6) **humorous**   funny   strange   amusing   serious

7) **rich**   wealthy   penniless   money   well

8) **plenty**   many   enough   few   quite

9) **raise**   high   up   increase   lower

10) **break**   repair   smash   crack   snap

b. Spell the Antonym

Example:	Complete the word on the right by filling in the missing letters. It is an antonym of the word on the left.
	war p ☐ ☐ c e

1. Think about the word on the left and its meaning. **War** means a fight between two opposing people or groups. Now look for a word that has the opposite meaning on the right. This clue may give the missing word straight away but, if not, proceed to the next step.

2. Try out letters from the alphabet in one of the spaces. The most obvious space to try is the first one. Only certain letters will fit. Some likely possibilities are **pa**, **pe**, **pi**, **pl**, **po**, **pr** or **pu**. This is a matter of trial and error.

p	a		c	e
p	e		c	e
p	i		c	e
p	l		c	e
p	o		c	e
p	r		c	e
p	u		c	e

If this does not give you the word then move to the next step.

3. Try out letters from the alphabet in the remaining space where only a few letters could possibly fit and make words. In the last part of the word there are limited letters that can work before **ce**. Only **a**, **e**, **i** and **n** will work. The only possible words are:

p	e	a	c	e
p	l	a	c	e
p	i	e	c	e
p	r	i	c	e
p	e	n	c	e

4. Now check the meanings of the words. The word that means the opposite of **war** is **peace**. As there are two words that are pronounced the same way, check the spelling. The correct spelling is **peace**.

The correct antonym is: peace

Exercise 8: 9 — Complete the word on the right by filling in the missing letters. It is an antonym of the word on the left:

1) **present** | | b | s | | n | t |

2) **rude** | p | o | l | | | e |

3) **wrong** | r | i | | | t |

4) **tight** | l | | | s | e |

5) **wide** | n | | r | | o | |

6) **cheer** | g | r | | | | n |

7) **defend** | a | | t | a | | k |

8) **export** | | | | p | o | r | t |

9) **light** | h | | | v | y |

10) **notice** | i | | n | o | | e |

Score

c. Mixed Examples

Exercise 8: 10 — Complete or underline the word on the right that is an antonym of the word on the left:

Score

1) **sharp**   spiky   blunt   pointed   jagged

2) **valiant**   cowardly   brave   noble   bold

3) **starve**   hungry   thirsty   eat   drink

4) **wise**   clever   intelligent   sensible   stupid

5) **alone**   solo   accompanied   lonely   only

6) **silly** | s | | n | s | | b | | e |

7) **cautious** | c | | r | | l | | s | s |

8) **cheap** | c | | s | t | l |

9) **eager** | | n | i | n | t | | r | e | s | t | | d |

10) **past** | p | r | | s | | n | t |

4. Homonyms

Homonyms are words that have the same spelling, but have different meanings.

Example: Which word will go equally well with both sets of words in the brackets?

(tip, end)   (place, spot)

position   finish   point   spike

One of these words is a homonym (has more than one meaning) and will match both sets of words in the brackets.

1. Think about the meanings of the words in each set of brackets and decide the difference between them.

(tip, end)

Tip or **end** as nouns mean the furthest part of an object.

(place, spot)

As nouns, **place** or **spot** mean a particular area on a map or object.

2. Now check the meaning of each word in turn to see if it matches either of the sets of words in the brackets:
   - **Position** is a noun that means a place where someone or something is located. This is a synonym of **place** and **spot**, but does not mean **tip** or **end**.
   - **Finish** is a noun that means the final part of something. This is a synonym of **end**, but does not mean **place** or **spot**.
   - **Spike** is a noun that means a thin, pointed piece of material. This is a synonym of **tip**, but does not mean **place** or **spot**.
   - **Point** is a noun that means the sharp end of an object and is also a particular spot or place in an area.

The correct homonym is: point

a. Level 1

Exercise 8: 11 Underline the one word which will link the two pairs of bracketed words:

1) (carer, nanny)　　　cure foster tend nurse
   (treat, heal)

2) (catch, stop)　　　paddock bowl green field
   (meadow, grassland)

3) (view, study)　　　watch follow track survey
   (timer, clock)

4) (price, cost)
   (attack, rush)
   storm bill charge lunge

5) (spot, mark)
   (mend, cover)
   dot patch repair smear

6) (tomb, vault)
   (serious, important)
   terrible critical grave awful

7) (near, alongside)
   (shut, lock)
   immediate close secure end

8) (centre, middle)
   (kidney, lung)
   core heart brain soul

9) (silly, joker)
   (trick, mislead)
   fool jester clown deceive

10) (harbour, pier)
    (outlet, socket)
    plug marina port inlet

Score

b. Level 2

Exercise 8: 12 Underline the one word which will link the two pairs of bracketed words:

1) (sharp, sour)
   (jealous, sullen)
   bitter   acid   harsh   spiteful   angry

2) (earth, dirt)   ground   muddy   soil
    (dirty, spoil)   stain   smear

3) (happy, pleased)   material   content   satisfied
    (subject, matter)   glad   mount

4) (flyer, poster)   notice   bill   spot
    (see, observe)   sign   mark

5) (light, soft)   still   peaceful   moderate
    (kind, tender)   gentle   pleasant

6) (catch, arrest)   abduct   movie   capture
    (record, show)   trap   imprisonment

7) (contest, game)   double   match   test
    (twin, copy)   lookalike   tournament

8) (give, award)   here   present   past
    (now, today)   gift   current

9) (sunny, light)   shining   intelligent   happy
    (smart, clever)   bright   aglow

10) (type, kind)   grade   shape   form
    (solve, fix)   order   sort

Score

Chapter Nine
CLOZE

Cloze exercises involve filling in missing words or parts of words that have been taken out of a passage of text. Cloze questions require an understanding of context (the words that surround the word) and vocabulary in order to find the correct words or part of a word that needs to be filled in.

Parts of Speech

It is important when doing a cloze activity to understand parts of speech as this can often help in finding missing words. A part of speech describes what a word does in the sentence. Many words work as different parts of speech depending on how they are used in a sentence.

For example:

David wanted to **train** (verb) to operate a locomotive so he could join a **train** (adjective) company and drive a **train** (noun) every day.

- Nouns – the name of a person, place or thing, e.g. **spoon**.
- Adjective – a word that describes a noun, e.g. **soup** spoon.
- Verb – a 'doing' word that shows activity, e.g. **ran**.
- Adverb – a word that describes a verb, e.g. ran **fast**.
- Conjunction or Connective – a joining word that links two parts of a sentence, e.g. **and** or **but**.
- Preposition – a word showing how words relate to each other. It can be thought of as showing position in time or space, e.g. came **after** dinner.
- Pronoun – a word that replaces a noun, e.g. **he** or **them**.

Context

Look at the meaning of the passage in which the missing word or word with missing letters is situated, as this can offer clues to solving cloze questions.

There are three types of cloze test:

Multiple-choice • **Word Bank** • **Missing Letters**

1. Multiple-choice

In **Multiple-choice** style questions there are three possibilities for each missing word in the cloze passage.

Example: Read the following cloze passage and identify the missing word from each multiple-choice option.

Michael Faraday was born in England in September 1791 and was a (**1.** teaching, pilot, scientist). He is (**2.** most, least, left) known for his discoveries in chemistry, electricity and magnetism. One of his most famous quotes is, "But still try, for who knows what is (**3.** possible, impossible, likely)." He (**4.** birth, born, died) in August 1867, aged (**5.** 73, 74, 75) years old.

© 2017 Stephen Curran

1. Read the passage and decide what it is about. This will provide clues for the missing words. This passage is about Michael Faraday. This method applies to all five questions but the following just looks at 1 and 2:

   Michael Faraday was born in England in September 1791 and was a (**1.** teaching, pilot, scientist). He is (**2.** most, least, left) known for his discoveries in chemistry, electricity and magnetism.

2. Two words do not fit in the sentence.

   Michael Faraday was born in England in September 1791 and was a **teaching**. He is **left** known for his discoveries in chemistry, electricity and magnetism.

   Teaching cannot have 'a' before it in a sentence.
   Left is an adjective and is the wrong part of speech.

3. Check for any words that do not fit the meaning.

   Michael Faraday was born in England in September 1791 and was a **pilot**. He is **least** known for his discoveries in chemistry, electricity and magnetism.

   Working with science is very different to being a **pilot**. A person would not be famous for being **least** known for something.

4. Try the remaining words in the sentence.

   Michael Faraday was born in England in September 1791 and was a **scientist**. He is **most** known for his discoveries in chemistry, electricity and magnetism.

   Both these words work in the sentence. The answers are:
   1. scientist   2. most

   Using the same process the other questions will give the following answers: **3. possible   4. died   5. 73**

Exercise 9: 1

Underline the correct words to complete the sentences:

1) (Swimming, Ran, Cycles) is a fun activity to do with (alone, friends, worker) in the (sand, field, pool).

2) (After, Before, During) going on holiday, everything needs to be (packed, thrown, crammed) neatly into a (folder, briefcase, suitcase).

3) The family went into a (cinema, restaurant, library), sat at a (chair, table, desk) and looked at the (menu, food, drink).

4) The (campers, hikers, scout) need to have a (tent, pond, bag) to sleep in, and food to cook over the (fire, smoke, wood).

5) To (learn, change, know) to play the piano, a person needs to (practise, practice, repeat) and spend a little time playing each (minute, day, hour).

6) A lot of children like (dinosaurs, dogs, reptiles), with a favourite being the Tyrannosaurus Rex, which is (fierce, gentle, soft) and (tall, short, high).

7) Football is a favourite (sport, ball, net) of many people, becoming a national sport with a (team, crowd, player) playing in the World (Cup, Trophy, Award).

8) Mount Etna is (widest, shortest, tallest) active volcano and is (founded, located, moved) in Sicily, Italy; it is in the (south, left, down) of the Alps.

9) The Greek god Atlas is known for (carrying, eating, making) the weight of the (universes, country, world) on his (head, shoulders, hands).

10) The messenger of the gods, Hermes, is always drawn with (buckles, laces, wings) on his shoes, so that he could travel to (many, few, no) places (quietly, quickly, slowly).

Cloze passages include various forms of text:
Historical • Biographical
General Knowledge • Literary Text Prose

a. Biographical

Exercise 9: 2 Select the correct words to complete the passage:

Score

Thomas Edison was born on 11th February 1847 in Milan, Ohio.

Edison 1) ☐ most / ☐ often / ☐ never entertained himself by taking things

2) ☐ together / ☐ apart / ☐ separate to see how they worked, so he decided to become

24 © 2017 Stephen Curran

an 3) ☐ inventor / ☐ assistant / ☐ educator . In 1870, Edison moved to New York City

and 4) ☐ began / ☐ finished / ☐ stopped working on the telegraph (a way of sending

messages electronically). He invented a version that could

5) ☐ look / ☐ received / ☐ send four messages at once. In 1877, Edison, with

6) ☐ help / ☐ difficult / ☐ timing , invented the phonograph. The phonograph was

a machine that recorded and played back sounds. In 1871, Edison

invented the light bulb, which is probably his 7) ☐ most / ☐ least / ☐ best well-

known invention. His inventions changed the 8) ☐ country / ☐ city / ☐ world

forever. They still influence the way we live 9) ☐ yesterday / ☐ today / ☐ tomorrow .

Edison worked until his 10) ☐ birth / ☐ death / ☐ birthday on 18 October 1931.

b. Biographical

Exercise 9: 3 Select the correct words to complete the passage:

Score

Pocahontas was one of the **1)** ☐ most ☐ known ☐ first Native Americans to

2) ☐ visit ☐ come ☐ live Britain. Her **3)** ☐ title ☐ name ☐ country means 'lively or

naughty one'. She was **4)** ☐ born ☐ died ☐ live in 1595 and came to Britain

to meet James I, who became **5)** ☐ prince ☐ lord ☐ king in 1603 after Queen

Elizabeth I died. Pocahontas **6)** ☐ helped ☐ stopped ☐ forced her people make

friends with colonists who had come to America from Britain. The

colonists were British people who travelled to **7)** ☐ other ☐ another ☐ different

26 © 2017 Stephen Curran

place to live there. She is famous for trying to keep the

8) ☐ piece / ☐ chaos / ☐ peace and being 9) ☐ brave / ☐ cowardly / ☐ heroine enough to leave

her home and cross the 10) ☐ place / ☐ city / ☐ ocean to Britain.

c. Historical

Exercise 9: 4 Select the correct words to complete the passage:

Score

The Tudors were the family that 1) ☐ lived / ☐ ruled / ☐ worked England between

1485 and 1603. There were 2) ☐ five / ☐ six / ☐ seven Tudor monarchs:

Henry VII, Henry VIII, Edward VI, Lady Jane Grey, Mary I and

Elizabeth I. They were 3) ☐ known / ☐ famous / ☐ called as the Tudors because

Henry VII was previously called Henry Tudor 4) ☐ before / ☐ during / ☐ after he

became 5) ☐ rule / ☐ lords / ☐ king . The monarch who had the

6) ☐ shortest / ☐ longest / ☐ least reign in this period was Lady Jane Grey, whose

reign lasted for 7) ☐ least / ☐ only / ☐ over nine days. The 8) ☐ most / ☐ longest / ☐ shortest

reigning 9) ☐ king / ☐ princess / ☐ monarch in this period was Elizabeth I, whose

reign lasted 45 years. Perhaps the most 10) ☐ known / ☐ celebrated / ☐ famous Tudor

monarch was Henry VIII who had six wives.

2. Word Bank

In **Word Bank** style questions there are a number of possible missing words at the top of the page. Words are chosen from this word bank to fill the spaces in the passage.

28 © 2017 Stephen Curran

Example: Choose the correct words from the word bank to fill each space in the cloze passage.

> only   cold   most
> shelter   rest

The giant panda is a solitary animal that spends **1)** _____ of the day eating and the **2)** _____ sleeping. Pandas almost **3)** _____ eat bamboo. They do not hibernate, but will **4)** _____ in caves or hollow trees in very **5)** _____ weather.

1. Read the whole passage and decide what the passage is about as this will provide clues for the missing words. This passage is about giant pandas.

2. Take each word in turn and try and establish its part of speech and meaning:

   - **only** could be an adverb or an adjective. As an adverb it could mean 'nothing more than', and as an adjective it means 'alone of its kind'.

   - **cold** is an adjective. It refers to low temperature.

   - **most** is an adverb and means a lot of something.

   - **shelter** can be a noun or a verb and refers to either protection or a place to shield from the weather.

© 2017 Stephen Curran

- **rest** can be a noun or a verb. As a verb it means 'to stop work' and as a noun it means the 'remaining part'.

3. Examine each cloze space and look for clues in the text that might help you find the correct word from the bank:

- 'spends _____ of the day' – The gap after **spends** shows it must be an adverb. This gives two choices: **only** does not work as **only** cannot be followed by **of**. It must be **most**.

- 'and the _____ sleeping' – This use of the article **the** means it must be a noun. This gives two options: **shelter** does not work as sleeping would not follow shelter. The remaining noun is **rest**.

- 'almost _____ eat bamboo' – This must be an adverb. The only remaining adverb is **only**.

- 'but will _____ in caves' – This must be a verb as it is followed by **in**. The only remaining verb is **shelter**.

- 'in very _____ weather' – This must be an adjective as it is describing the weather. The only option is **cold**.

The passage would therefore read:

The giant panda is a solitary animal that spends **most** of the day eating and the **rest** sleeping. Pandas almost **only** eat bamboo. They do not hibernate, but will **shelter** in caves or hollow trees in very **cold** weather.

a. Historical

Exercise 9: 5 — Choose the correct words from the word bank to complete the passage below:

| bathing | elderly | poor | family | used |
| between | children | rich | sleep | husband |

The Aztecs lived in central Mexico **1)** _____ the 14th and 16th centuries. **2)** _____ life was very important to the Aztecs. The **3)** _____ worked outside of the home, whereas the wife worked inside the house. The **4)** _____ attended school or helped out at home. The **5)** _____ members of the family were well taken care of and respected within society. There was a big difference between the rich and the **6)** _____ . The **7)** _____ lived in homes made of stone or brick and had a separate **8)** _____ room. The poor lived in huts that had one or two rooms – one room to **9)** _____ in and the rest of the space was **10)** _____ for cooking, eating and as a palace for shrines to the gods.

b. General Knowledge

Exercise 9: 6 Choose the correct words from the word bank to complete the passage below:

Score

| hour | year | air | few | safest |
| called | move | travel | speeds | stay |

A tornado is a very fast moving, spinning tube of

1) _____ that touches the ground and the cloud above.

Tornadoes can also be **2)** _____ twisters. Most tornadoes

have wind **3)** _____ of less than 100 miles per

4) _____ , but some tornadoes can reach speeds of over

300 miles per hour. Tornadoes mostly only travel a

5) _____ miles, however extreme twisters can

6) _____ over 100 miles. The country that has the most

tornadoes every year is the USA, which has an average of 1,200

tornadoes per **7)** _____ . Tornadoes can cause trees to

fall down or **8)** _____ , and can also damage buildings.

It is best to **9)** _____ in basements or other underground

areas during a tornado and it is also **10)** _____ to stay

away from windows.

c. General Knowledge

Exercise 9: 7 Choose the correct words from the word bank to complete the passage below:

Score

| Pacific | Atlantic | second | god | covered |
| third | deepest | over | water | sea |

About 70% of the Earth's surface is **1)** _____ by **2)** _____ . The largest ocean is the **3)** _____ , which covers around 30% of the Earth's surface. The name 'Pacific Ocean' comes from Latin, meaning 'peaceful **4)** _____ '. The **5)** _____ known area of the Earth's oceans is the Mariana Trench, which is 11km deep. The **6)** _____ largest ocean is the **7)** _____ Ocean, which covers **8)** _____ 21% of the Earth's surface. It's name is a reference to the Titan God, Atlas, from Greek mythology, who was the **9)** _____ of endurance. The **10)** _____ largest ocean on Earth is the Indian Ocean, covering 14% of the Earth's surface.

3. Missing Letters

In **Missing Letters** questions, the cloze passage includes a number of words where letters have to be provided to complete the word.

Consonants and Vowels

It can be helpful to split up consonants and vowels when trying out various letters in spaces. Working through the alphabet is useful and does not take long.
Remember that:

- There are 21 consonants and some, such as **q**, **x** and **z**, are rarely used. This narrows it down to 18 regularly used consonants.

- There are five vowels: **a**, **e**, **i**, **o** and **u**.

Letter Combinations

When doing missing letter questions, remember that there are some rules that can help you identify missing letters:

- Certain consonants cannot be next to each other, e.g. **p** cannot be followed by **q** to make **pq**.

- Some same vowels cannot be next to each other, e.g. **u** cannot follow **u** to make **uu**.

- Some letters always go together, e.g. **qu**.

- Some vowels often go together, e.g. **ee**, **ea**, **ia**, etc.

- Some consonants often join together to form a different sound, e.g. **th** or **ph**.

- Most words begin with a consonant and end with a consonant, e.g. **boat**.

- A small number of words begin and end with a vowel, e.g. **era**.

Example: Fill in the missing letters to complete the passage below:

Antarctica is the southernmost 1) [c][o][ ][t][ ][n][ ][n][t] and the site of the 2) [s][ ][ ][t][h] pole. It is 3) [a][ ][m][o][ ][t] uninhabited and 4) [c][o][m][ ][l][e][t][ ][l][y] covered in ice. There are many species of wildlife there, 5) [i][ ][c][l][ ][d][ ][n][g] penguins.

1. Read the passage carefully and decide what it is about. This passage is about Antarctica.

2. Look at the context of each word (words around it) and look for clues in the parts of speech:

   - 'Antarctica is the southernmost [c][o][ ][t][ ][n][ ][n][t]' - this word must be a noun and the context is helpful. What is Antarctica? It is a 'continent'.

   - 'the site of the [s][ ][ ][t][h] pole' – this word must be an adjective and must be a direction. There is only one direction beginning with 's', so the word must be 'south'.

- 'It is [a]_[m][o]_[t] uninhabited' – this word must be an adverb as it describes 'uninhabited'. Looking at the ending [o]_[t], the missing letter must be 's'. The word must be 'almost'.

- '[c][o][m]_[l][e][t]_[l][y] covered in ice' – this word must be an adverb as it ends in 'ly'. Antarctica is totally covered in ice. A synonym for 'totally' is 'completely'. This must be the answer.

- 'There are many species of wildlife there, [i]_[c][l]_[d]_[n][g] penguins' – this must be a preposition and looking at the ending _[n][g], the missing letter must be 'i' to give 'ing'. Looking at the beginning [i]_[c] the missing letter must be 'n'. The word must be 'including'.

3. Read the passage to check all the missing letters that have been filled in make sensible words that fit the context. The passage will read:

Antarctica is the southernmost **continent** and the site of the **south** pole. It is **almost** uninhabited and **completely** covered in ice. There are many species of wildlife there, **including** penguins.

The correct words are:

1) continent 2) south 3) almost
4) completely 5) including

a. Literary Text Prose

Exercise 9: 8 Fill in the missing letters to complete the passage below:

Score

The dragon, on 1) `h e a r i n g` the

2) `a p p r o a c h i n g` footsteps, made the

3) `b e g i n n i n g` of a courteous

4) `e f f o r t` to rise. But when he saw it was a Boy,

he set his eyebrows firmly.

"Now don't you hit me," he said; "or bung stones, or

5) `s q u i r t` water, or anything. I won't have it, I tell you!"

"Not goin' to hit you," said the Boy wearily,

6) `d r o p p i n g` on the grass beside the

7) `b e a s t` : "and don't, for goodness' sake,

8) `k e e p` on saying 'Don't'; I 9) `h e a r` so much

of it, and it's boring, and makes me 10) `t i r e d`."

An extract from *The Reluctant Dragon* by Kenneth Grahame (1859-1932).

b. General Knowledge

Exercise 9: 9 Fill in the missing letters to complete the passage below:

Score

The Statue of Liberty is 1) **l _ c _ t _ _** on

Liberty Island in the New York 2) **h _ r b _ _ r** .

It was a gift from the people of France to the United States.

It was 3) **a s _ e m _ l _ d** on a base after being

made in France and sent to the United States in

4) **c r _ t _ s** . It was dedicated on 28th October 1886

and was 5) **d e _ i _ n e _** by the French sculptor

Frederic Bartholdi. The form of the statue is 6) **b _ s _ d**

on the Roman 7) **_ o _ d e s _** of liberty – Libertas.

She holds a torch and a tablet. The 8) **o _ f _ i _ _ a l**

name of the Statue of Liberty is 'Liberty Enlightening the World'.

There are copies of the 9) **s t _ t _ _** in Paris, Las Vegas

and many other 10) **c _ t _ _ s** around the world.

38 © 2017 Stephen Curran

c. Literary Text Prose

Exercise 9: 10

Fill in the missing letters to complete the passage below:

Heidi's aunt had 1) [a] [ ] [r] [i] [e] [ ] in the meantime with Peter, who was 2) [e] [ ] [g] [ ] [r] to see what was going to 3) [h] [ ] [p] [ ] [e] [n].

"Good-day to you, uncle," said Deta as she 4) [a] [ ] [p] [r] [ ] [a] [ ] [h] [e] [d].

"This is Tobias's and Adelheid's child. You won't be able to 5) [r] [e] [ ] [e] [ ] [b] [ ] [r] her, because last time you saw her she was 6) [s] [ ] [a] [r] [ ] [e] [ ] [y] a year old."

"Why do you bring her here?" asked the uncle, and 7) [t] [u] [ ] [n] [ ] [n] [ ] to Peter he said: "Get away and bring my goats. How late you are 8) [a] [ ] [r] [ ] [ ] [d] [y]!"

Peter obeyed and 9) [d] [ ] [s] [a] [p] [p] [ ] [r] [e] [d] on the spot; the uncle had looked at him in such a 10) [m] [ ] [n] [ ] [e] [r] that he was glad to go.

An extract from *Heidi* by Johanna Spyri (1827-1901).

Chapter Ten
SYNTAX

Syntax means arranging of words and phrases to create well-formed sentences. Syntax questions usually involve unscrambling some jumbled words and forming them into a sentence.

Four things are helpful when forming correct sentences:

1. A sentence is a group of words that makes sense on its own. For example:

    'Biscuits, cheese, pickle, shop on Wednesday' is not a sentence because it is incomplete. It is just a list and a day and it is not clear what is meant.
    'I wrote an essay for my school teacher.' is a sentence because it is a complete statement.

2. A sentence should begin with a capital letter and end with a full stop. Sometimes these are included in questions to assist you when unscrambling a sentence.

3. A sentence should always include a verb (a doing word) and a subject (the thing or person doing the verb). It is important to look for these as it can help you reorder a sentence. For example:

    *'The **children** (subject) **built** (verb) sandcastles on the beach.'*

4. Sentences can contain two or more parts and can be separated by a conjunction or a preposition such as *'and'* or *'before'*. For example:

'Bobby bought five stamps at a corner shop **and** some sweets in the supermarket.'

'Vanessa went to breakfast club **before** she set off for school.'

Syntax questions are of four types:

Words Changing Places • Basic Ordering Selecting a Specific Word • Selecting the Extra Word

1. Words Changing Places

Example: Which two words have to change place to make this sentence read correctly?

Today, I need shopping go to.

1. Read the sentence and try and identify what it is about. This sentence seems to be about the act of shopping.
2. Now look for the point in the sentence where it fails to make sense. The phrase 'shopping go to' does not make sense as 'to' would not end a sentence. The words that need to change places are 'shopping' and 'to'.
3. Check the words work in their new positions in the sentence.

'Today, I need to go shopping.'

Exercise 10: 1 Underline the two words which should change place in order to make these sentences read correctly:

1) his needs to complete Jonathan homework.

2) Nigel is the mowing lawn.

3) Keira sing to likes.

4) The picture painted a painter of the sea.

5) Mark offered of make everybody a cup to tea.

6) Caitlyn came first in the day at sports race.

7) The grass pigs ran around in the guinea.

8) Our class teacher gave us Christmas at presents.

9) Dad is going to drive my to me nan's.

10) The cinema is closed two for weeks.

Score

2. Basic Ordering

Example: Unscramble the following sentence so that it makes complete sense:

motorbike. bought shiny The man a

1. Check whether a word that has a capital letter has been provided. This will indicate which word starts the sentence. 'The' does have a capital letter so this word begins the sentence. If there is no capital letter it is still important to identify the word most likely to start the sentence.

2. Check whether a word with punctuation after it has been provided. This will indicate which word ends the sentence. 'motorbike.' is followed by a full stop so this word ends the sentence.

3. Think about the subject of the sentence as this may give some clues to forming a correct sentence. This is about someone buying something.

4. If 'the' begins this sentence, only 'man' or 'motorbike' can follow this particular word. This is likely to be followed with 'bought', so the likely phrase is 'The man bought'. The word 'shiny' must be connected to 'motorbike' so 'shiny motorbike' go together.

5. Filling in the rest of the sentence is not very difficult. 'The man bought' must be followed by 'a shiny motorbike'.

The correct sentence is:

'The man bought a shiny motorbike.'

Exercise 10: 2 Unscramble the following words to form complete sentences:

1) interview got job. The girl the for an

2) how a learn calculator. to child needed use The to

3) an Shauna important is writing letter.

4) telephone. the Sheila answering is

5) I bake like cake. a would to

6) the the all we went theme in on park rollercoasters of

   _____

7) three milk bottles milkman of delivered the

   _____

8) subjects many the tutor different taught

   _____

9) delivered parcel the a postman

   _____

10) bowling I best and went my friend

    _____

Score

3. Selecting a Specific Word

Example: Unscramble and identify the fifth word in this sentence:

staying in hotel I am a

1. Read the scrambled sentence and try to identify what it is about. This sentence is obviously about a hotel.

2. Identify which words must go together. There are two word combinations in this sentence; 'I am' links with 'staying' and 'in a hotel' will go together.

3. Now combine the phrases to form a sentence.
   This sentence would therefore read:
   'I am staying in a hotel.'

4. Look for the fifth word in the sentence:

   The fifth word in the sentence is: **a**

Exercise 10: 3 Unscramble these words to make a sentence and underline the requested word:

1) 7th word: wants farm to go my to the niece

2) 3rd word: backpack very my full is

3) 6th word: lunch all of eaten I have my

4) 1st word: of pictures drawn lots has Annabel

5) 8th word: look to the ordering need at before you menu

6) 5th word: the books surrounded woman is by

7) 3rd word: a can cousin my drive tractor

8) 2nd word: carriages had eight train the

9) 4th word: messy bedroom your very is

10) 6th word: day family out enjoyed the their

4. Selecting the Extra Word

Example: Unscramble these words to make a sentence and identify the one word which cannot fit into the sentence.

ran the snake the garden slithered around

1. Read the scrambled sentence and decide what it is about. As this sentence contains the noun 'snake' and the verbs 'ran' and 'slithered', it has something to do with a snake and with movement.

2. Try to link words that are likely to go together. Focus on the words 'around', 'the' and 'garden'; the phrase 'around the garden' is possible.

3. The sentence is likely to begin with the word 'the' as this is used twice and the noun 'snake' is likely to be linked to 'the' as it is the subject of the sentence.
   The phrases made so far are:
   'The snake' and 'around the garden'.

4. There are two possible verbs, 'ran' and 'slithered', that could come after the noun 'snake'. As snakes do not run, 'slithered' is the better option.
   Therefore the sentence must read:
   'The snake slithered around the garden.'
   It is helpful to number the words to show the extra word:

	5	2	1	6	3	4
ran	the	snake	the	garden	slithered	around

5. If the whole sentence is put together it will read:
   'The snake slithered around the garden'.
   The word that will not fit into this sentence is: **ran**

a. Level 1

Exercise 10: 4 Unscramble these words and underline the one extraneous word:

1) chocolate chip cookies I bought bough some

2) cycled child ride the school to

3) Sandra two boarded to aeroplane an Spain

4) be the two full emptied to bin needs

5) the won Amanda bee on spelling

6) fill a helped I stopped Dad form out

7) party my having is a had sister sleepover

8) weekend friends for went camping the fore four the

9) enclosure of got garden its out elephant the

10) a the for monkey photograph poised posed

Score

b. Level 2

Exercise 10: 5 Unscramble these words and underline the one extraneous word:

1) some the Uncle petrol in to car put John think needed

2) threw flew gaggle geese house my a yesterday of over

3) the clapped the show at of the end the audience

4) you cast tells the the names the programme of the

5) knew new had lock door we on our front a fitted

6) that is inside outside day van there ice-cream stops every an

7) her on the had sad face man a his look

8) to the the too was girl to shop trusted go

9) local they to girl the rugby join club wants the

10) the handed the of out teacher year reports end off

Score

Chapter Eleven
COMPREHENSION

Comprehension involves understanding a passage of text and answering questions about it.
This involves learning about the following:

Fiction & Non-fiction • **Forms of Prose**
Comprehension Skills • **The Five W's**
The Three Question Types

1. Fiction & Non-fiction

Passages of text break into two basic categories:

- **Fiction** is text that is not true and has been created from a person's imagination.

- **Non-fiction** is text that is true and is based upon real events.

Example: Give an example of a piece of fiction.

Katy's name was Katy Carr. She lived in the town of Burnet, which wasn't a very big town, but was growing as fast as it knew how. The house she lived in stood on the edge of the town. It was a large square house, white, with green blinds, and had a porch in front.

This is fiction. It is an extract from *What Katy Did* by Susan Coolidge (1835-1905).

Example: Give an example of a piece of non-fiction.

Cannes is a seaport and city in France on the Mediterranean coastline. It is a popular holiday destination in the French Riviera. The world-famous Cannes Film Festival is held there annually every May.

This is non-fiction. It is an extract about *Cannes*.

Exercise 11: 1

Identify whether these extracts of text are fiction or non-fiction:

Score

1) *Once upon a time there was an old cat, called Mrs Tabitha Twitchit, who was an anxious parent. She used to lose her kittens continually, and whenever they were lost they were always up to mischief! On baking day she decided to shut them up in a cupboard. She caught Moppet and Mittens, but she could not find Tom.*

   Is this fiction or non-fiction? _____

2) <u>*River Thames - Friday 27th May to Friday 29th July 1768*</u>
   Moderate to fair weather. At 11am I hoisted the flag and, as Captain, took charge of the ship, Endeavor. She was lying at Deptford Yard. Up to the 21st of July we spent time fitting out the ship, taking on board stores and provisions. The same day we sailed from Deptford and anchored in Gallions reach, where we remained until the 30th July.

   Is this fiction or non-fiction? _____

3) *"I shan't be able to think in ten minutes, make it half an hour," said H.O. His real name is Horace Octavius, but we call him H.O. for short, because of the advertisement for Hornby's Oats. It's not so very long ago he was afraid to pass the billboard where it says 'Eat H.O.' in big letters. We thought this was very funny.*

   Is this fiction or non-fiction? _____

4) *As soon as the moon rose above the horizon, he saw her through his telescope. He did not let the moon out of his sight at all and followed her course across the sky. He thought of his friends, who had now landed on the moon, who he might not see again.*

   Is this fiction or non-fiction? _____

5) *17th January 1623 - The very first thing that I can remember at an early age was my youngest brother being held in his nurse's arms. He was nine months and two days younger than me and the last of my parents' children to be born.*

   Is this fiction or non-fiction? _____

6) *Edward Jenner was born in Berkeley, Gloucestershire, in 1749. He became a doctor in 1772 and was the first doctor to vaccinate people against smallpox, which was a dangerous disease. He wrote a book about this discovery and became the most famous doctor in the world at that time. He died in 1823.*

Is this fiction or non-fiction? _____

7) *At the moment when our story closes, Heidi and Peter are sitting in grandmother's hut. The little girl has so many interesting things to tell and Peter is trying so hard not to miss anything she says.*
   Finally, the grandmother says, "Heidi, please read me a song of thanksgiving and praise. I feel that I must praise and thank the Lord for the blessings he has brought to us all!"

Is this fiction or non-fiction? _____

8) *The Great Barrier Reef is a large coral reef extending for 1,616 miles along the north-east coast of Australia. It is the world's largest living structure containing millions of tiny organisms. It is so big it can be seen from space.*

Is this fiction or non-fiction? _____

9) *Mr Brownlow spent day after day filling the mind of his adopted child, Oliver, with stores of knowledge. He became increasingly attached to him as Oliver grew into a fine young man with many prospects.*

Is this fiction or non-fiction? _____

10) *Elizabeth Fry was born on 21st May 1780 to a rich family. Her mother taught her that rich people should help others through charity work. She visited prisoners who were treated extremely badly at that time. Her work led to prison reform by the government. She died in 1845.*

Is this fiction or non-fiction? _____

2. Forms of Prose

Prose describes all forms of text that are not poetry. The basic categories forms of prose are as follows:

Narrative

This has a storyline with a beginning, middle and end. The events of the story are often based around a main character and sometimes a narrator tells the story. It is usually fictional but can be based on true events such as historical fiction. It includes novels, short stories, fables, legends, myths, fantasy and fairy stories.

This is an adapted extract of narrative text from *Indian Tales* by Rudyard Kipling (1865-1936).

> *His name was Charlie Mears; he was the only son of his mother who was a widow, and he lived in the north of London. He came into the City every day to work in a bank. He was twenty years old and was very ambitious. I met him in a public house and he told me of his desire to be a writer. His mother did not encourage his writing, so he asked, "Do you mind if I stay here and write all this evening? I won't interrupt you. There's no place for me to write at home."*

Biography or Autobiography

This tells the story of someone's life. If a person tells their own story it is called an autobiography. If somebody else tells their story it is called a biography.

This is an autobiographical extract from Autobiography of a Yogi by Paramhansa Yogananda (1893-1952).

> *My name is Mukunda Lal Ghosh. I was born in the last decade of the nineteenth century, and spent my first eight years in my birthplace of Gorakhpur in north-east India. I was the fourth of eight children: four boys and four girls. I was the second boy to be born.*

This is a biographical extract about Queen Elizabeth I.

Elizabeth I was born in 1533 and was the daughter of King Henry VIII and Anne Boleyn, the second of Henry's wives. She became queen in 1558 and never married. She reigned for so long that the period of her life became known as 'the Elizabethan era'. She died in 1603 and was buried in Westminster Abbey.

Factual Text

This kind of text contains truthful information without giving an opinion. It can include textbooks, encyclopedias, leaflets, recipes, catalogues, directories and manuals.

This is a piece of factual text about *Hockey*.

Hockey is a game played with a ball by two opposing sides, using hooked or bent sticks, with which each side attempts to drive the ball into the other's goal. Field hockey is played on grass with 11 players in each team, including the goalie. The game can also be played on ice with 6 players per team.

Letters or Emails

These are a form of communication from one person or group to another. They can be formal (a letter of complaint to a company) or informal (a personal letter to a friend). Text messages are another way of communicating using prose.

This is an extract of a letter from Pliny the Younger (61-113).

To Cornelius Tacitus,

You will laugh (and you are quite welcome) when I tell you that your old friend has turned into a sportsman. I have hunted and killed three large boars. "What!" you exclaim, "Surely not Pliny!", yes, me! However, while hunting I also enjoyed my favourite activity, lazing around and watching the fishermen at their nets.

Farewell, Pliny.

Journals or Diaries

These are a way of recording daily events or personal experiences. They often include a date or time of day for each entry and can include very personal information and thoughts. Journals are normally more detailed than diaries.

This is an extract from *The Diary of a U-Boat Commander* by an anonymous author.

> <u>2nd November 1914</u> - *I am off tonight for a six-day trip. It has been a great piece of luck. It has been arranged by the Naval Authorities; and two officers from this squadron could go. There were 130 candidates, so we drew lots; as usual I was lucky and drew one of the two chances. It should be intensely interesting.*

Plays or Film Scripts

These are written versions of plays or films. They tell the actors and directors how to perform the play or create the film. They contain the names of characters, their dialogue, stage directions and important descriptive action.

This is an extract from *The Verge* by Susan Glaspell (1876-1948).

> ANTHONY: But please do close the door. This stormy air is not good for the plants.
> HARRY: But fresh air is just the thing for me! Now, what do you mean, Anthony, by not answering the phone?
> ANTHONY: Mrs Archer told me not to.
> HARRY: Told you not to answer the phone to me?
> ANTHONY: Not you especially—but nobody.

Example: Identify the form of prose below.

John Logie Baird was born in 1888 in Scotland. He helped invent the television and was the first to show TV pictures in people's homes. Baird used boxes, biscuit tins, sewing needles, card, and the motor from an electric fan to make his first TV in 1924.

Answer: This form of prose is biographical as it is about the inventor John Logie Baird's life.

Exercise 11: 2

Identify the form of prose in the following extracts:

Score

1) <u>5th January 1660</u> - *I went to my office, where the money was expected from the tax office. It was not there, but was promised to be sent this afternoon. I dined with Mr Shepley at Admiral Sir Edward Montagu's lodgings. We ate large portions of turkey pie. Then I went to my office again and the excise money had finally arrived.*

   This form of prose is _____.

2) *I was the youngest son, and the youngest child but two, and was born in Boston, New England. My mother was Abiah Folger, the daughter of Peter Folger. He was one of the first settlers of New England, and is mentioned honourably in Cotton Mather's church history of New England. The entry describes him as "a godly, learned Englishman," if I remember the words rightly.*

   This form of prose is _____.

3) *My dear Fox,*
   When I arrived here on Tuesday I found to my great grief and surprise, a letter on my table which I had written to you about a fortnight ago. The foolish porter had not bothered to send it.

   This form of prose is _____.

4) *An anaconda is an aquatic boa constrictor. It inhabits the swamps and rivers of the dense forests of tropical South America. It is the largest of all snakes, growing to over 30 foot in length and can devour large land mammals.*

   This form of prose is _____.

5) *Once on a dark winter's day, the yellow fog hung thick and heavy in the streets of London. The street lamps were lit and the shop windows glowed as they do at night. An odd-looking little girl sat in a horse-drawn cab with her father and was driven rather slowly through the streets.*

   This form of prose is _____.

6) SCENE II. Athens. QUINCE'S house.
[Enter Quince, Snug, Bottom, Flute, Snout and Starveling]
QUINCE: Is all our company here?
BOTTOM: You were best to call them generally, man by man, according to the script.
QUINCE: Here is the scroll of every man's name, which is thought fit, through all Athens, to play in our interlude before the duke and the duchess, on his wedding-day at night.

This form of prose is _____.

7) *Nelson Mandela was born on 18th July 1918. As an adult, he was arrested and imprisoned a few times for speaking out against the South African government, which treated black people unfairly. His was imprisoned for life in 1964 but was finally in 1990. In 1994, he became President of South Africa. He died in Johannesburg on 5th December 2013.*

This form of prose is _____.

8) *Above, the sky was bluest of the blue. Out into the brimming sun-bathed world I sped from the school house, free of lessons, free of discipline and correction, for one day at least. My legs ran by themselves, and though I heard my name called faint and shrill from behind, there was no stopping me. It was only Harold, I decided, and his legs, though shorter than mine, were strong enough to catch up with me.*

This form of prose is _____.

9) <u>*Monday, 17th*</u> *- Today is the first day of school. These three months of vacation in the country have passed like a dream. This morning my mother took me to the Baretti schoolhouse to enrol me into the third elementary class. All I could think of was the countryside and I went to school unwillingly.*

This form of prose is _____.

10) *Amethyst is a violet or purple variety of quartz. The semiprecious stone is often used in jewellery and is the traditional birthstone for people born in February. There is an allocated birthstone for every month of the year.*

This form of prose is _____.

3. Comprehension Skills

When first looking at a passage of text, always remember to:
- **Read Without 'Voicing'** - This means to read the passage by silently 'mouthing the text' without using your voice. This helps concentration when reading and stops the mind from wandering.
- **Read Actively** - When reading look for information in the text that will give clues to what it is about.
- **Answer Correctly** - Read multiple-choice answer options very carefully before selecting an answer.

It is then possible to scan the text. This means to quickly look through the text without reading everything in detail in order to find the answers.

4. The Five W's

Five basic questions can be asked to explore information contained in the text:

1. **Where does it take place?** Look out for the locations that are mentioned in the text and how they are described.
2. **When does it take place?** In what period of history is the passage set? Are there any other clues about the time of day, year, season, or how long any action takes place for?
3. **Who is involved?** Identify any key characters and look for descriptions of them.
4. **What happens?** Look for the main actions that occur in the passage. Is there one key event?
5. **Why does it happen?** What does the key event tell us about the passage? Do the characters give any more clues to the meaning of the passage?

Example: Read the following passage about evacuees and answer the five 'w' questions:
1) Where does it take place?
2) When does it take place?
3) Who is involved?
4) What happens?
5) Why does it happen?

When World War II began in September 1939, the British government expected the country would be attacked by German planes. Air raid shelters were built and poison gas masks were given out for protection. School lessons continued as usual, but children took part in 'air raid drills' and learned how to put on their gas mask. At night, children slept in the air raid shelters.

Michael was 9 when the war began and his family was split up. His father left home to join the army and his mother and older sister, Anne, went to work in the local factory. Bombing began in June 1940, destroying many buildings and Michael played with excitement on the bombsites. He had to walk over fallen bricks and broken glass in the streets to get to school. Food and clothing were rationed due to shortages and Michael received hardly any toys for Christmas, and not many sweets either. Michael's friend Peter, along with thousands of other children, was evacuated from London and sent to the countryside.

Notes on text:
Rationed - each person was only allowed a certain amount
Evacuated - remove from a dangerous place to a safer place

1) Where does it take place?

List the locations mentioned - It takes place Britain; in London and the countryside.

Note any descriptions given - London has 'bombsites', many destroyed buildings and air raid shelters.

2) When does it take place?

Note the period of history - It takes place during World War II.

List any specific dates or time periods - The war began in September 1939 and the bombing began in June 1940.

3) **Who is involved?**
List the key characters - The passage is mainly about Michael, his family and his friend Peter.
Describe the main features of the characters - Michael is 9 years old and enjoys playing like a normal child.

4) **What happens?**
List the main events - The start of the war, the bombing of London and the evacuation.
What is the main event that takes place? The bombing that began in June 1940 is the main event.

5) **Why does it happen?**
What reasons does the passage give for the events taking place? A worldwide war was taking place, meaning Britain was being attacked.

Exercise 11: 3

Read the following passage, *The Little Match Girl*, and answer the following questions:

It is extremely cold, snowy and dark; the last night of the year. A poor, little girl, with nothing on her head, walks the streets. She wears slippers that belong to her mother and are far too big for her. A carriage rattles past while she crosses the road. She jumps out of the way and both slippers fall off. (4)

A boy runs away with one slipper, yelling, "It's so big, my baby sister could fit inside it!"

She searches for the other slipper, but it has fallen through the grating and she cannot reach it. (8)

The little girl's bare feet grow red and blue with cold. She carries a bundle of matches in her hand. No one has bought anything from her all day. She is hungry and shivers. Snowflakes fall on her long yellow hair, which curls prettily over her neck. Lights shine from all the windows and there is a wonderful smell of roast goose wafting through the street. (12)

She sits at a corner between two houses, draws up her little feet, but feels even colder. The girl does not dare go home because she has not sold any matches. Her father will beat her; and besides, it is cold at home too as the wind whistles through the rickety roof. (16)

Her tiny hands are numb. She decides to draw a match from the bundle and strike it against the wall to warm her hands. Scratch! The match splutters and burns into a warm, bright flame, like a little candle. For a moment, it seems to her as if she sits before a grand fireplace. The little girl holds out the match to warm her feet too. The flame suddenly goes out and she is left holding the burned-out match. (20) (24)

She strikes another and its light shines on the wall. It seems as if the wall is transparent and she can see into a room. There is a table laid with china on a white tablecloth. A steaming roast goose, stuffed with apples and dried plums, sits at the centre. Suddenly, the goose hops down from the dish and waddles along the floor, towards the little girl. Then the match goes out, and only the thick, damp wall is before her. (28) (32)

She lights another and finds herself under a beautiful Christmas tree with hundreds of candles burning on its branches. The little girl stretches her hands towards them; then the match goes out. The Christmas tree lights rise higher and higher until they become stars. One falls from the sky in a long line of fire. (36)

*   "Someone is dying," she cries.*
Her long-dead grandmother once told her that when a star falls from the sky, a dead person's spirit goes up to God. She rubs another match against the wall and in its light, stands her grandmother, shining like the sun. (40)

*   "Grandmother!" calls the child. "Take me with you! I know you'll leave when the match burns out. You'll go away like the fireplace, the goose and the tree!"* (44)

She hastily rubs the whole bundle of matches, attempting to make her grandmother stay. The matches burn so brightly that it seems like daytime. Her beautiful grandmother takes the little girl up in her arms, and they both fly high through the light to a place where there is no more hunger, care or cold – they are with God in heaven. (48)

At the corner between the two houses sits the girl, with red cheeks and a smiling mouth, frozen to death. The sun rises on the little body that lays there with the burned matches in her hand. (52)

Adapted from the story by Hans Christian Andersen (1805-1875).

Where

1) Where was the little girl when she lost her slipper?
   - a) Sitting in front of a fireplace.
   - b) Crossing the road.
   - c) Lying on the ground.
   - d) Dinning at a large dinner table.

2) Where did the grandmother take the little girl?
   - a) Home
   - b) To the fire
   - c) Heaven
   - d) To get something to eat

When

3) When did the story take place?
   - a) New Year's Eve
   - b) 30th December
   - c) Christmas Eve
   - d) New Year's Day

4) At what time of day does the story end?
   - a) Dusk
   - b) Night time
   - c) Dawn
   - d) Midday

Who

5) What was the little girl's hair like?
   - a) Blonde and straight
   - b) Brown and straight
   - c) Blonde and curly
   - d) Brown and curly

6) Which character is the little girl afraid of?
   - a) The boy
   - b) Her father
   - c) Her grandmother
   - d) Her mother

What

7) What becomes see-through in the story?
   - a) The wall
   - b) The matches
   - c) The Christmas tree
   - d) The goose

8) What did the Christmas tree lights turn into?
   - a) Matches
   - b) Flames
   - c) Candles
   - d) Stars

Why

9) Why was the little girl smiling in line 53?
   - a) She had finally joined her grandmother.
   - b) She was so cold.
   - c) She was no longer hungry.
   - d) The sun was shining.

10) Why was it a problem that the girl had not sold any matches?
    - a) She wasted them all on herself.
    - b) Her usual customers were unable to find her.
    - c) It meant she had not made any money.
    - d) Everybody would now be cold.

5. The Three Question Types

There are only three types of comprehension question. They are as follows:

- **Factual Information** – This involves finding straightforward facts from the text. It is sometimes described as finding information 'on the line'.

- **Contextual Understanding** – This requires understanding what comes before and after the relevant part of the text. The answer is not always obvious. This is often called finding the answer 'between the lines'.

- **Evaluative Opinion** – This requires an understanding of the whole passage and what it is about. This is the most difficult of all the skills. It can be described as looking for the answer 'beyond the lines'.

Example:
> Read the following passage from *The Wolf and the Kid* and answer these three questions:
> 1) What did the Kid ask the Wolf to do before he ate him? (Factual)
> 2) Why did the Kid run around calling for his mother? (Contextual)
> 3) What is the message of this story? (Evaluative)

There was a little Kid goat who though he could take care of himself. One evening, as the goats left the field, his mother called him. He ignored her and kept nibbling grass. When he eventually looked up, the flock was gone. (4)
The sun set, shadows lengthened and the wind whistled. The Kid thought of the terrible Wolf and shivered. He ran about wildly, bleating for his mother. Nearby, in a clump of trees, he saw the Wolf!

The Kid knew there was little hope.

"Please, Mr Wolf," he stuttered, "I know you're going to eat me, but first, sing to me, for I want to dance and be happy for a little longer." (8)

The Wolf liked the idea of some music before dinner, so he sang a merry tune and the Kid leaped and hopped joyfully. (12)

As the flock moved homeward, the Shepherd Dogs heard the Wolf's distant mealtime song. They raced back to the field. The Wolf stopped singing and ran away with the Dogs at his heels. He realised he was a fool for following the Kid's request, instead of just eating him! (16)

Adapted from a story by Aesop (620-564BCE).

1) What did the Kid ask the Wolf to do before he ate him?

The answer to this question can be found easily in the text. The Kid asks the Wolf to sing him a song before eating him. This can be found in line 9.

2) Why did the Kid run around calling for his mother?

This question is a little more difficult because it involves understanding the text. The answer is found by understanding what occurs before and after the event in the question. The Kid ran around calling for his mother because he realised that he should have gone home with her and now he is in danger of being eaten by a wolf.

3) What is the message of this story?

This question is more difficult because it involves understanding the meaning of the story and giving a viewpoint on it. The message of this story is that when you have decided to do something you should not become distracted because the opportunity might not come again. The Wolf wanted to eat the Kid, but got side-tracked by singing and in the end, he failed to have his meal.

Exercise 11: 4

Read the following passage, *Becoming a Knight*, and answer the following questions:

There were three kinds of soldiers during the Middle Ages (700-1400CE): foot soldiers or infantry, archers who were skilled with a bow and arrow, and heavily armoured soldiers, called knights, who fought on horseback. (4)

Young men could become a knight in two ways. Firstly, a man could prove himself by being brave during a battle. If a soldier fought particularly well he might receive a knighthood from a lord, another knight or even the king. The second way was for a young man to be an apprentice to a knight and gain the title by working and training hard. (8)

Even though many young men dreamed of becoming knights, it was expensive and only a few could afford it. They had to buy weapons, armour and a powerful war horse. This meant knights usually came from upper-class families whose fathers were already serving knights. (12)

A boy who wanted to become a knight would often join a knight's household as a page boy when he was seven years old. He would serve meals to the knight, clean his clothes and carry messages to people. By living as a member of the castle staff he would learn how to behave at the king's court. His martial arts training would begin by learning how to hunt with a hawk. He would also be given lessons in how to fight and would practice with wooden swords and shields. It would also include learning how to ride a horse without using his hands and carry a lance (a long pole with a sharp steel point) at the same time. He would be taught how to read and to play the lute. (16) (20) (24)

Between the ages of thirteen and fifteen he could be appointed squire (meaning 'shield bearer'). He would now look after the knight's horses, clean his weapons and armour, and attend battles with the knight. A squire might be asked to fight, so he trained with proper weapons and was given lessons by the knight in how to use them. He would (28) (32) *often be permitted to carry a small sword and shield to show his status as a squire or 'knight in training'. He had to be physically fit and develop his strength. To prepare for the day when he became a knight, a squire had to practise his horsemanship and improve his jousting skills by attacking a wooden dummy called a quintain with a lance. He also had to learn to fight with a sword while mounted on a horse. He was taught how to attack and defend castles. His training normally lasted five or six years. If a squire showed he had courage and skill, he could become a knight at the age of twenty-one or after fighting bravely on the battlefield. Most rich knights would have many enthusiastic page boys and squires willing to serve them.* (36) (40) (44)

A young squire would receive the title of knight at a 'dubbing ceremony'. Beforehand, he would take a special bath to clean himself and spend the night alone praying. During the ceremony, a knight, lord or the king would briefly touch the flat blade of his sword on both shoulders of the kneeling squire. The new knight would swear a promise to protect the king and the church. In return he would be given a sword, a shield bearing his family's crest and some riding spurs. Knights were required to serve 40 days each year fighting for the king. In exchange for this, a knight could be given money from battles, lands of his own and a position in the king's court. (48) (52)

Notes on text:
Jousting (line 37) – a sport where two opponents try to knock each other off their horses using lances
Crest (line 52) – a special symbol that represents an important family
Spurs (line 52) – a sharp piece of metal placed on the heels of riding boots to direct a horse

Factual Information
1) What weapon did the archers use?

   ☐ a) Sword
   ☐ b) Bow and arrow
   ☐ c) Gun
   ☐ d) Lance

2) How old would a boy have to be before he could become a knight?

    ☐ a) 7
    ☐ b) 13
    ☐ c) 15
    ☐ d) 21

3) Which of the following duties would a squire do?

    ☐ a) Clean the knight's clothes
    ☐ b) Serve meals to the knight
    ☐ c) Clean the knight's weapons
    ☐ d) Carry messages to people

4) At what stage in his training would a boy be given proper weapons?

    ☐ a) Page boy
    ☐ b) Squire
    ☐ c) Knight
    ☐ d) Lord

Contextual Understanding

5) What was the main difference between knights and other soldiers?

    ☐ a) Knights rode on horses.
    ☐ b) Knights used swords.
    ☐ c) Knights went through years of training.
    ☐ d) Knights could hunt.

6) How would 'riding spurs' (line 52) help a knight?

    ☐ a) They would give the knight better control of his horse.
    ☐ b) They would make him rich.
    ☐ c) They would make his horse more attractive.
    ☐ d) They would help the knight defend himself from attackers.

7) Why was a dubbing ceremony so important?

    ☐ a) There was a chance the king could be present.
    ☐ b) The boy would receive gifts.
    ☐ c) It was the moment a boy officially became a knight.
    ☐ d) The boy would have a bath for the occasion.

8) What does the word 'apprentice' (line 9) mean in this context?

    ☐ a) Someone who has finally become a knight.
    ☐ b) A brave fighter.
    ☐ c) Someone who cannot afford to become a knight.
    ☐ d) A person who is learning from someone more skilled than them.

9) Why was it difficult for a poorer man to become a knight?

    ☐ a) They did not know any knights.
    ☐ b) They had no experience of fighting in battles.
    ☐ c) They did not have their own squire.
    ☐ d) The equipment was very expensive.

Evaluative Opinion

10) Why was the title of 'knight' so important and admired?

    ☐ a) They were very good at looking after horses.
    ☐ b) Knights could fight well.
    ☐ c) They were servants to lords and the king.
    ☐ d) It was the highest honour an ordinary man could achieve.

Score

Notes

Answers

11+ Verbal Activity Year 4/5 Workbook 3

Chapter Eight
Classification

Exercise 8: 1
1) metre
2) lion
3) plane
4) car
5) school
6) Germany
7) Tuesday
8) butterfly
9) banana
10) shop

Exercise 8: 2
1) twist
2) wage
3) window
4) train
5) read
6) joy
7) gnaw
8) permit
9) match
10) many

Exercise 8: 3
1) straight
2) big
3) earth
4) usual
5) sad
6) curtain
7) good
8) past
9) happy
10) plastic

Exercise 8: 4
1) talking
2) person
3) slow
4) fits
5) type
6) smile
7) aged
8) survivor
9) Autumn
10) mirror

Exercise 8: 5
1) dash
2) phantom
3) field
4) gutter
5) coast
6) serious
7) match
8) fury
9) servant
10) reply

Exercise 8: 6
1) famous
2) infant
3) glance
4) brush
5) troops
6) giggle
7) pause
8) harbour
9) scare
10) cooker

Exercise 8: 7
1) ruin
2) teacher
3) round
4) pirate
5) healed
6) start
7) tear
8) clown
9) weird
10) terrific

Exercise 8: 8
1) crouch
2) below
3) capture
4) warm
5) admit
6) serious
7) penniless
8) few
9) lower
10) repair

Exercise 8: 9
1) absent
2) polite
3) right
4) loose
5) narrow
6) groan
7) attack
8) import
9) heavy
10) ignore

11+ Verbal Activity
Year 4/5 Workbook 3

Answers

Exercise 8: 10
1) blunt
2) cowardly
3) eat
4) stupid
5) accompanied
6) sensible
7) careless
8) costly
9) uninterested
10) present

Exercise 8: 11
1) nurse
2) field
3) watch
4) charge
5) patch
6) grave
7) close
8) heart
9) fool
10) port

Exercise 8: 12
1) bitter
2) soil
3) content
4) notice
5) gentle
6) capture
7) match
8) present
9) bright
10) sort

Chapter Nine
Cloze
Exercise 9: 1
1) Swimming, friends, pool
2) Before, packed, suitcase
3) restaurant, table, menu
4) campers, tent, fire
5) learn, practise, day
6) dinosaurs, fierce, tall
7) sport, team, Cup
8) tallest, located, south
9) carrying, world, shoulders
10) wings, many, quickly

Exercise 9: 2
1) often
2) apart
3) inventor
4) began
5) send
6) help
7) most
8) world
9) today
10) death

Exercise 9: 3
1) first
2) visit
3) name
4) born
5) king
6) helped
7) another
8) peace
9) brave
10) ocean

Exercise 9: 4
1) ruled
2) six
3) known
4) before
5) king
6) shortest
7) only
8) longest
9) monarch
10) famous

Exercise 9: 5
1) between
2) Family
3) husband
4) children
5) elderly
6) poor
7) rich
8) bathing
9) sleep
10) used

Exercise 9: 6
1) air
2) called
3) speeds
4) hour
5) few
6) travel
7) year
8) move
9) stay
10) safest

Answers

*11+ Verbal Activity
Year 4/5 Workbook 3*

Exercise 9: 7
1) covered
2) water
3) Pacific
4) sea
5) deepest
6) second
7) Atlantic
8) over
9) god
10) third

Exercise 9: 8
1) hearing
2) approaching
3) beginning
4) effort
5) squirt
6) dropping
7) beast
8) keep
9) hear
10) tired

Exercise 9: 9
1) located
2) harbour
3) assembled
4) crates
5) designed
6) based
7) goddess
8) official
9) statue
10) cities

Exercise 9: 10
1) arrived
2) eager
3) happen
4) approached
5) remember
6) scarcely
7) turning
8) already
9) disappeared
10) manner

Chapter Ten
Syntax

Exercise 10: 1
1) his & Jonathan
2) the & mowing
3) sing & likes
4) picture & painter
5) of & to
6) day & race
7) grass & guinea
8) Christmas & presents
9) my & me
10) two & for

Exercise 10: 2
1) The girl got an interview for the job.
2) The child needed to learn how to use a
    calculator.
3) Shauna is writing an important letter.
4) Sheila is answering the telephone.
5) I would like to bake a cake.

11+ Verbal Activity
Year 4/5 Workbook 3

Answers

6) We went on all of the rollercoasters in the theme park.
7) The milkman delivered three bottles of milk.
8) The tutor taught many different subjects.
9) The postman delivered a parcel.
10) My best friend and I went bowling.

Exercise 10: 3
1) the
2) is
3) my
4) Annabel
5) before
6) by
7) can
8) train
9) very
10) out

Exercise 10: 4
1) bough
2) ride
3) two
4) two
5) on
6) stopped
7) had
8) fore
9) garden
10) poised

Exercise 10: 5
1) think
2) threw
3) the
4) the
5) knew

6) inside
7) her
8) too
9) they
10) off

Chapter Eleven
Comprehension
Exercise 11: 1
1) Fiction - An adapted extract from The Roly Poly Pudding by Beatrix Potter (1866-1943)
2) Non-fiction - An adapted extract from Captain Cook's Journal During His First Voyage Round the World (1768-1771)
3) Fiction - An adapted extract from The Story of the Treasure Seekers by Edith Nesbit (1858-1924)
4) Fiction - An adapted extract from From the Earth to the Moon by Jules Verne (1828-1905)
5) Non-fiction - An adapted extract from The Diary of John Evelyn by John Evelyn (1620-1706)
6) Non-fiction - An extract about Edward Jenner
7) Fiction - An adapted extract from Heidi by Johanna Spyri (1827-1901)
8) Non-fiction - An extract about The Great Barrier Reef

Answers

*11+ Verbal Activity
Year 4/5 Workbook 3*

9) Fiction - An adapted extract from Oliver Twist by Charles Dickens (1812-1870)
10) Non-fiction - An extract about Elizabeth Fry

Exercise 11: 2
1) Journal or Diary - An adapted extract from The Diary of Samuel Pepys by Samuel Pepys (1633-1703)
2) Autobiography - An adapted extract from Autobiography of Benjamin Franklin by Benjamin Franklin (1706-1790)
3) Letter - An adapted extract from The Life and Letters of Charles Darwin by Charles Darwin (1809-1882)
4) Factual - An extract about anacondas
5) Narrative - An adapted extract from A Little Princess by Frances Hodgson Burnett (1849-1924)
6) Play or Film Script - An adapted extract from A Midsummer Nights Dream by Shakespeare (1564-1616)
7) Biography - An extract about Nelson Mandela
8) Narrative - An adapted extract from The Golden Age by Kenneth Grahame (1859-1932)
9) Journal or Diary - An adapted extract from An Italian Schoolboy's Journal by Edmondo De Amicis (1846-1908)
10) Factual - An extract about amethyst

Exercise 11: 3
1) b
2) c
3) a
4) c
5) c
6) b
7) a
8) d
9) a
10) c

Exercise 11: 4
1) b
2) d
3) c
4) b
5) a
6) a
7) c
8) d
9) d
10) d

PROGRESS CHARTS

8. CLASSIFICATION

Shade in your score for each exercise on the graph. Add up for your total score.

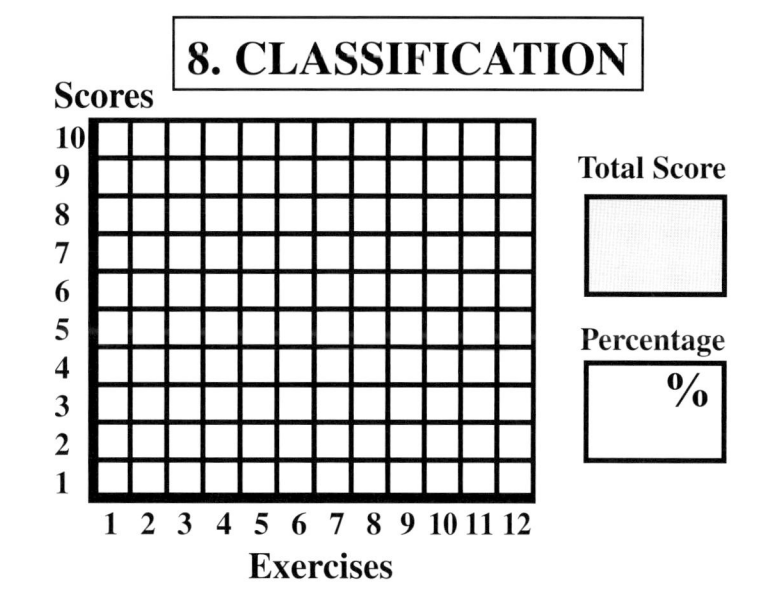

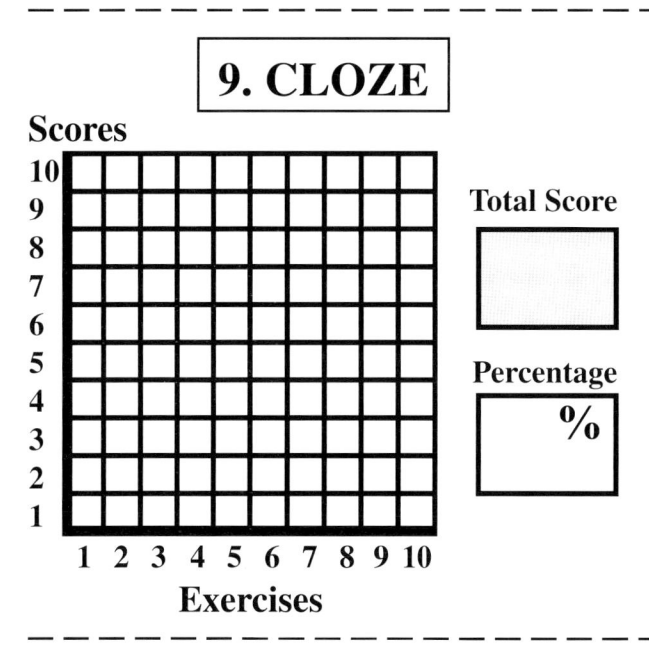

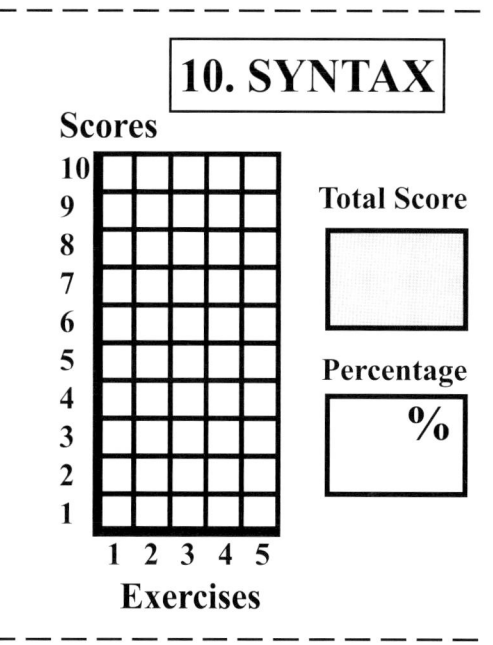

Scores (1–10) / Exercises (1–12)

Total Score

Percentage %

9. CLOZE

Scores (1–10) / Exercises (1–10)

Total Score

Percentage %

10. SYNTAX

Scores (1–10) / Exercises (1–5)

Total Score

Percentage %

11. COMPREHENSION

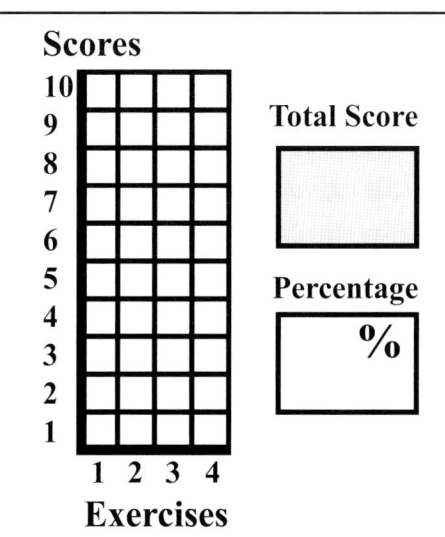

Scores (1–10) / Exercises (1–4)

Total Score

Percentage %

Add up the percentages and divide by 4

Overall Percentage %

© 2017 Stephen Curran

CERTIFICATE OF

ACHIEVEMENT

This certifies

_____

has successfully completed

11+ Verbal Activity Year 4/5

WORKBOOK 3

Overall percentage score achieved [   ] %

Comment _____

_____

Signed _____
(teacher/parent/guardian)

Date _____